Baby Gorillas

Julie Murray

Abdo Kids Junior
is an Imprint of Abdo Kids
abdobooks.com

Abdo
BABY ANIMALS
Kids

abdobooks.com

Published by Abdo Kids, a division of ABDO, P.O. Box 398166, Minneapolis, Minnesota 55439. Copyright © 2019 by Abdo Consulting Group, Inc. International copyrights reserved in all countries. No part of this book may be reproduced in any form without written permission from the publisher. Abdo Kids Junior™ is a trademark and logo of Abdo Kids.

Printed in the United States of America, North Mankato, Minnesota.

102018

012019

THIS BOOK CONTAINS RECYCLED MATERIALS

Photo Credits: Alamy, Minden Pictures, Shutterstock

Production Contributors: Teddy Borth, Jennie Forsberg, Grace Hansen

Design Contributors: Christina Doffing, Candice Keimig, Dorothy Toth

Library of Congress Control Number: 2018945716

Publisher's Cataloging-in-Publication Data

Names: Murray, Julie, author.
Title: Baby gorillas / by Julie Murray.
Description: Minneapolis, Minnesota : Abdo Kids, 2019 | Series: Baby animals set 2 |
    Includes glossary, index and online resources (page 24).
Identifiers: ISBN 9781532181634 (lib. bdg.) | ISBN 9781532182617 (ebook) |
    ISBN 9781532183102 (Read-to-me ebook)
Subjects: LCSH: Gorilla--Juvenile literature. | Baby animals--Juvenile literature. |
    Zoo animals--Infancy--Juvenile literature.
Classification: DDC 599.884--dc23

Table of Contents

Baby Gorillas 4

Watch a Mountain
Gorilla Grow! 22

Glossary. 23

Index 24

Abdo Kids Code. 24

Baby Gorillas

A **female** gorilla has one baby at a time. She can also have twins.

The baby weighs three to four pounds (1.4 to 1.8 kg). It has very little hair.

It drinks its mother's milk.

The baby cannot walk.

The mother carries it.

It grows quickly. Now it can ride on its mother's back.

It begins to eat plants.

The baby is eight months old.

It learns to walk.

The baby loves to play.

It runs and climbs.

It has fun with others in the **troop**.

Watch a Mountain Gorilla Grow!

newborn

1 year

4 years

10 years

Glossary

female
a girl animal that can have young.

troop
a group of gorillas that live together.

Index

climbing 18

food 8, 14

growth 12

hair 6

mother 4, 8, 10, 12

movement 10, 12, 16, 18

size 6

troop 20

Visit **abdokids.com** and use this code to access crafts, games, videos, and more!

Abdo Kids Code:
BBK1634